THE GREAT BOOK OF ANIMAL KNOWLEDGE

BOBCATS

Bob-tailed Cats of North America

All Rights Reserved. All written content in this book may NOT be reproduced in any form or by any means, including scanning, photocopying, or otherwise without prior written permission of the copyright holder. Copyright © 2014

Some Rights Reserved. All photographs contained in this book are under the Creative Commons license and can be copied and redistributed in any medium or format for any purpose, even commercially. However, you must give appropriate credit, provide a link to the license, and indicate if changes were made.

Introduction

Photo by Land Between The Lakes KY/TN (flickr.com/lblkytn), as licensed under CC BY-SA 2.0 Generic

Bobcats are a member of the cat family. Bobcats resemble house cats; however, they are actually a kind of lynx which is also part of the cat family. They are fierce hunters that can take down big prey.

What Bobcats Look Like

Bobcats look very similar to house cats. They have big eyes, furry bodies, whiskers on their face, and ears that stand up on their head. Bobcats also have sharp paws. They look like overgrown house cats.

Fur & Tail

Photo by Rennett Stowe (flickr.com/ tomsaint), as licensed under CC BY 2.0 Generic

The fur color of bobcats ranges from beige to brown. The spots or lines on their fur are either dark brown or black. Bobcats get their name from their tails. Their tails are short and it looks like it has been bobbed, therefore they are called bobcats.

Size & Weight

Bobcats are about two times the size of a house cat. They grow about 2-3 feet long from their head to the base of their tail. Their tails grow only 4-7 inches. Bobcats weigh 11-30 pounds.

Where Bobcats Live

Photo by Rennett Stowe (flickr.com/tomsaint), as licensed under CC BY 2.0 Generic

Bobcats can be found across the USA and some can be found in Canada and Mexico. They can survive in lots of different environments; from cold mountains to hot deserts. However, bobcats prefer rocky hills with many plants.

What Bobcats Eat

Photo by U.S. Fish and Wildlife Service Northeast Region (flickr.com/usfwsnortheast), as licensed under CC BY 2.0 Generic

Bobcats, like all animals in the cat family, are carnivores. This means that they have to eat meat to survive. Bobcats usually hunt and eat rabbits, hares, mice, squirrels, birds, and sometimes even deer! Also, in places where bobcats live close to farms, they sometimes kill livestock such as chickens and sheep.

Hunting

Photo by Miguel Vieira (flickr.com/miguelvieira), as licensed under CC BY 2.0 Generic

Bobcats are strong, fierce hunters. Their hunting skills allow them to take down prey about two times their size! Bobcats hunt with stealth. They creep close to their prey before pouncing on them from up to 10 feet away, and landing with a killer blow.

Senses

Bobcats have an excellent sense of hearing and sight. Bobcats usually hunt when it's dark so these two senses are very important for them. They also have a good sense of smell.

Behavior

Like most cats, bobcats are solitary animals. They prefer to live alone and aren't usually seen together. They are also secretive animals. It's not easy to find a bobcat in the wild, despite the fact that there are lots of bobcats in lots of different environments. This is because they try to avoid being seen. Bobcats are also nocturnal animals. This means that they are more active during nighttime than daytime.

Sounds

Bobcats make several different sounds. They growl and snarl. Bobcats also make different sounds that can be described as sounding like a baby or a woman screaming.

Territory

Bobcats are territorial animals. Each bobcat has their own territory which they mark with urine and distinct claw marks on trees. Male bobcats have larger territories than females, and their territories sometimes overlap. However, male territories do not overlap with other male territories.

Dens

Bobcats have several dens around their territory. These dens are hollow trees or narrow openings in rocks. During the day when bobcats are less active, they rest in these dens.

Breeding

The bobcat breeding season is during late winter. Female bobcats are pregnant for 8 to 10 weeks. After this time she will give birth to up to 6 baby bobcats in one of her dens. Male bobcats do not help raise the young.

Baby Bobcats

Baby bobcats are born blind and only open their eyes after 10 days. They drink their mother's milk until they are old enough to start eating meat. Young bobcats will stay with their mother for 9-12 months. They learn how to hunt during this time before leaving their mother and finding their own territory.

Predators

Despite being a fierce hunter, bobcats are sometimes preyed on by bigger animals. Their main predators are cougars and wolves. Baby bobcats are also in danger of owls, coyotes, and some other predators snatching them while their mother goes out to hunt.

Humans and Bobcats

Photo by Don DeBold (flickr.com/ddebold), as licensed under CC BY 2.0 Generic

Bobcats don't usually attack humans, but there are some rare occasions when a rabid bobcat will attack. Bobcats are considered pests in some places because they kill and eat livestock and pets. In other places, bobcats are hunted and trapped for their soft fur.

Relatives

Bobcats are part of the felidae family, or cat family. They are related to house cats, lions, tigers, jaguars and all other cats. The closest relatives to the bobcats are the lynxes. In fact, bobcats are actually a species of lynx.

Canadian Lynx

Canadian Lynxes are found in Canada and Northern USA. It is easy to confuse a bobcat for a Canadian lynx. The two animals look very similar and they can both be found along the USA/Canada border. There are some differences between the two animals. Canadian lynxes have larger paws, longer legs, longer ear tufts and some other differences.

Eurasian Lynx

The Eurasian lynx is the largest of the lynx family. They can be found in northern, central, and Eastern Europe; also in Siberia and eastern Asia. Eurasian Lynxes also have bigger paws and longer legs than bobcats. This helps them walk in the thick snow and hunt their favorite food, snowshoe hares.

Iberian Lynx

The Iberian Lynx can be found in Spain and Portugal. Iberian Lynxes are expert rabbit hunters. Sadly, diseases are killing lots of the rabbits that the Iberian Lynx relies on as its main food source. Therefore, the Iberian Lynx populations are declining and they are now an endangered species.

Subspecies

Although bobcats are one species, there are several differences between bobcats living in different locations. These are usually just tiny differences like their color or what they eat. There are thirteen subspecies of bobcat that can be found across North America. These all have different scientific names like L. Rufus rufus, L. Rufus gigas, and L. Rufus texenis.

Get the next book in this series!

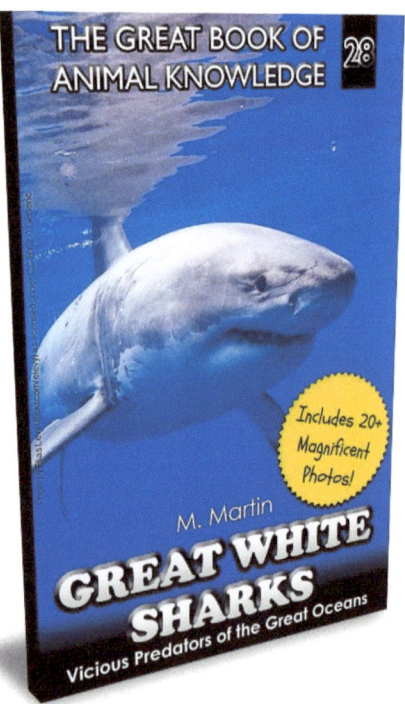

GREAT WHITE SHARKS: Vicious Predators of the Great Oceans

Log on to Facebook.com/GazelleCB for more info

Tip: Use the key-phrase "The Great Book of Animal Knowledge" when searching for books in this series.

For more information about our books, discounts and updates, please Like us on FaceBook!

Facebook.com/GazelleCB

CPSIA information can be obtained
at www.ICGtesting.com
Printed in the USA
BVHW011750080523
663791BV00001B/5